Getting Around Town

Sandy Phan

Consultants

Shelley Scudder
Gifted Education Teacher
Broward County Schools

Caryn Williams, M.S.Ed.
Madison County Schools
Huntsville, AL

Publishing Credits

Dona Herweck Rice, *Editor-in-Chief*
Lee Aucoin, *Creative Director*
Torrey Maloof, *Editor*
Diana Kenney, M.A.Ed., NBCT,
Associate Education Editor
Marissa Rodriguez, *Designer*
Stephanie Reid, *Photo Editor*
Rachelle Cracchiolo, M.S.Ed., Publisher

Image Credits: Cover & pp. 1, 5, 7, 17 Alamy; p. 21 BigStock; p. 19 Dreamstime; p. 9 The Granger Collection; p. 15 Google Maps; pp. 4, 10–11, 18–19 iStockphoto; p. 21 (top) Diana Kenney; pp. 6, 8, 12–13, 14, 24 Mapping Specialists; All other images from Shutterstock.

Teacher Created Materials
5301 Oceanus Drive
Huntington Beach, CA 92649-1030
http://www.tcmpub.com

ISBN 978-1-4333-6975-9

Printed in China
Nordica.012019.CA21801586

Table of Contents

Where To?

People travel all over town. They travel to school, work, and the store. They travel to many other places, too. People use maps to get where they are going.

Maps help people know where to drive.

Map Maker

A cartographer (kahr-¯OG-ruh-fur) is a person who makes maps.

This cartographer is making a map.

Give Me Directions!

Maps have a **compass rose**. This is a design that shows directions. The directions are *north*, *south*, *east*, and *west*. A map might show you that your school is east of your house.

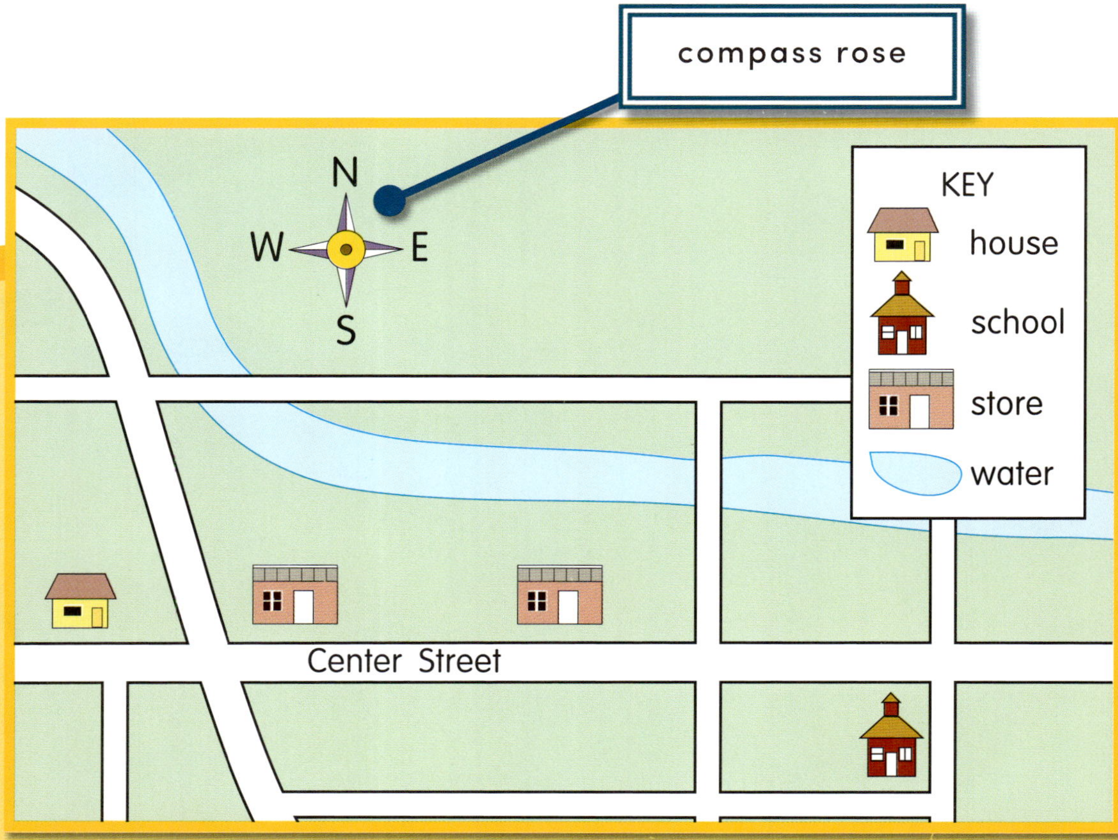

Two friends look at a map in a city.

Using Maps

A town map is a picture of a whole town. The **key** tells you what the lines, shapes, and colors mean. Each **symbol** (SIM-buhl) shows a place in town.

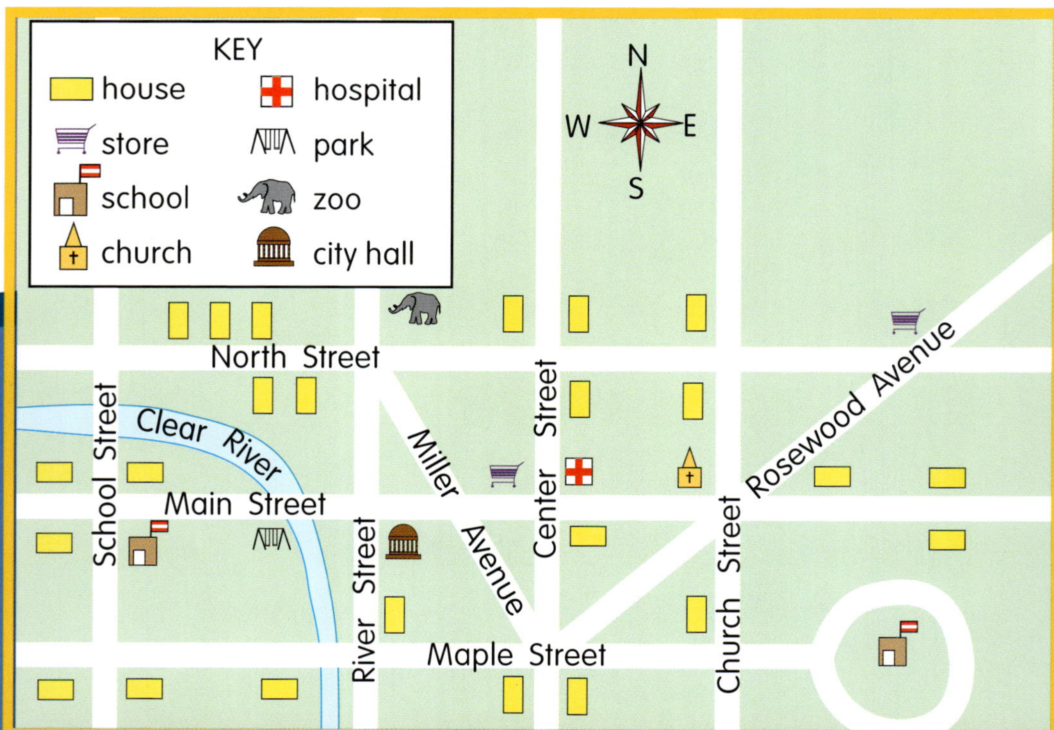

This map has a key at the top.

A Map of the Stars

Long ago, people used the stars as a map. The star patterns helped them find their way.

A sailor finds his way by looking at the stars.

The lines on a map show roads, from large highways to small streets. People use these roads to get from place to place. Blue lines and shapes on maps show areas of water.

Important Places

Map symbols show important places. A bus may show a bus stop. A table may show a picnic area.

This is a river.

How Far?

Real places and the **distance** between them are drawn much smaller on maps than they really are. A map's **scale** tells you how to measure distances on the map. One inch may **equal** (EE-kwuhl) one mile.

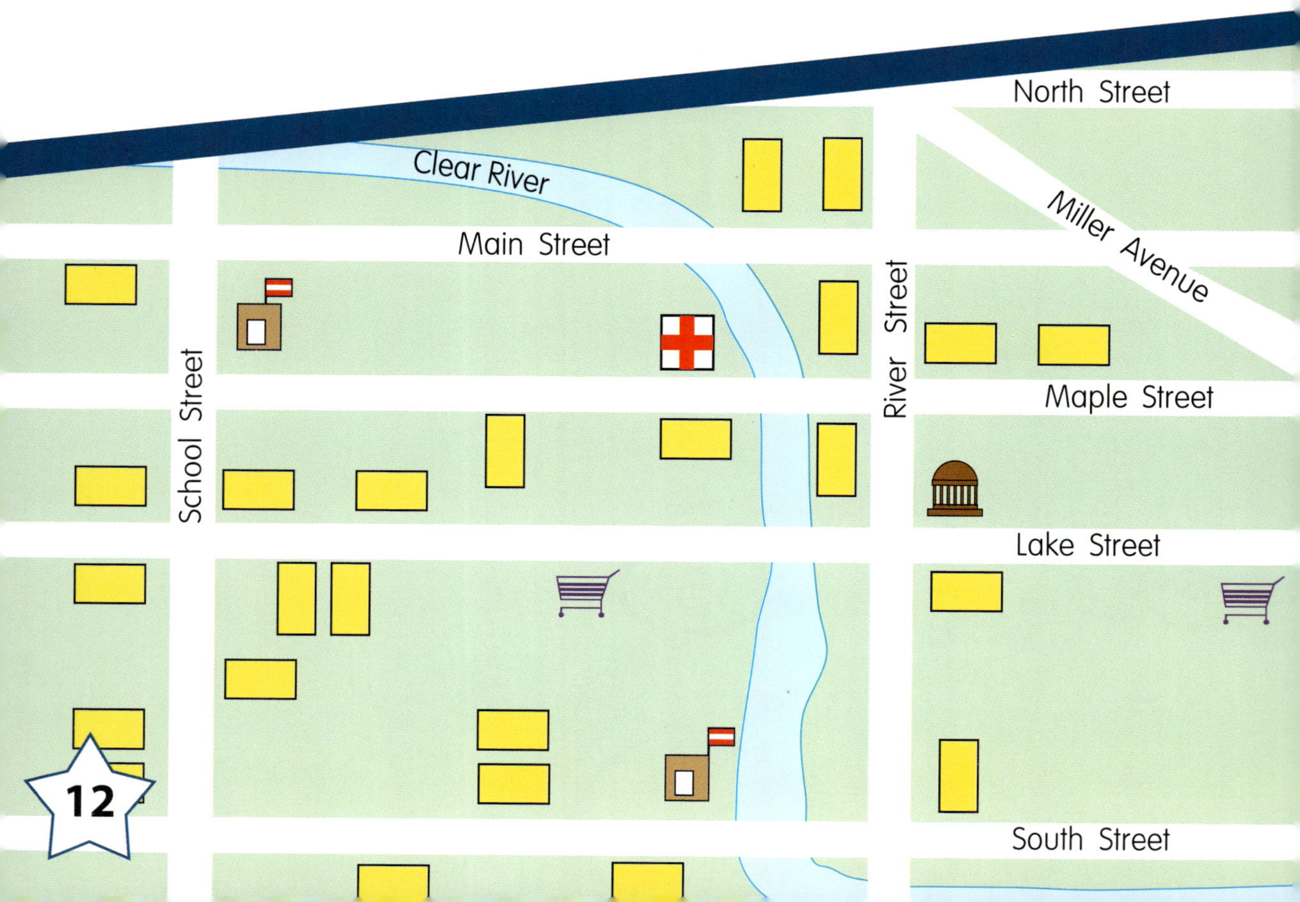

Large Scale

On a map of the world, one inch can equal 1,000 miles!

This is a scale.

On the Grid

A map may be drawn on a **grid** with lines. A grid has letters or numbers along two sides. There is a rectangle where each letter and number meet. You can find a place by looking for its rectangle.

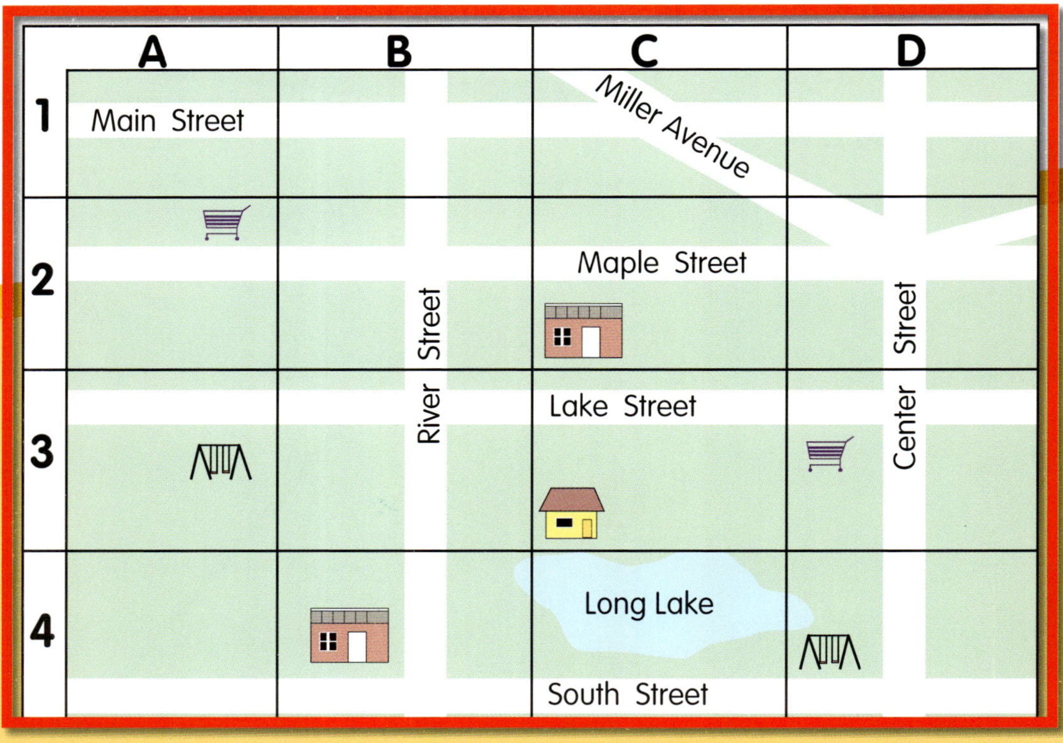

This map has a grid. It shows a house in C3.

Computer Maps

Many people use computers for maps. The computer helps them know where to go.

This map is from a computer.

Which Way?

Maps help people give directions. Maps can help you decide whether you should go north, south, east, or west. You will know where to turn and how far to travel.

This invitation has a map.

This boy shows his grandpa a place on a map.

Become a Map Master!

All towns are different. But every town has a map. The parts of the map will help you know where you are. Learn how to read maps so you can get around any town!

A girl and her dad use a map on their trip.

Map It!

Draw a map of your town. Include the places below. Add a compass rose and a key, too. Then tell a friend how to get from your house to a place in town.

Places

- city hall
- fire station
- hospital
- library
- my house
- my school
- park
- police station
- post office
- supermarket

This boy draws a map of his town.

Glossary

compass rose—a design on a map that shows north, south, east, and west

distance—the amount of space between two places

equal—the same

grid—a pattern of lines that cross each other to form rectangles

key—a list that tells what the symbols on a map mean

scale—a line used to measure distances on a map

symbol—a picture or a shape on a map that stands for a real place or thing

Index

Your Turn!

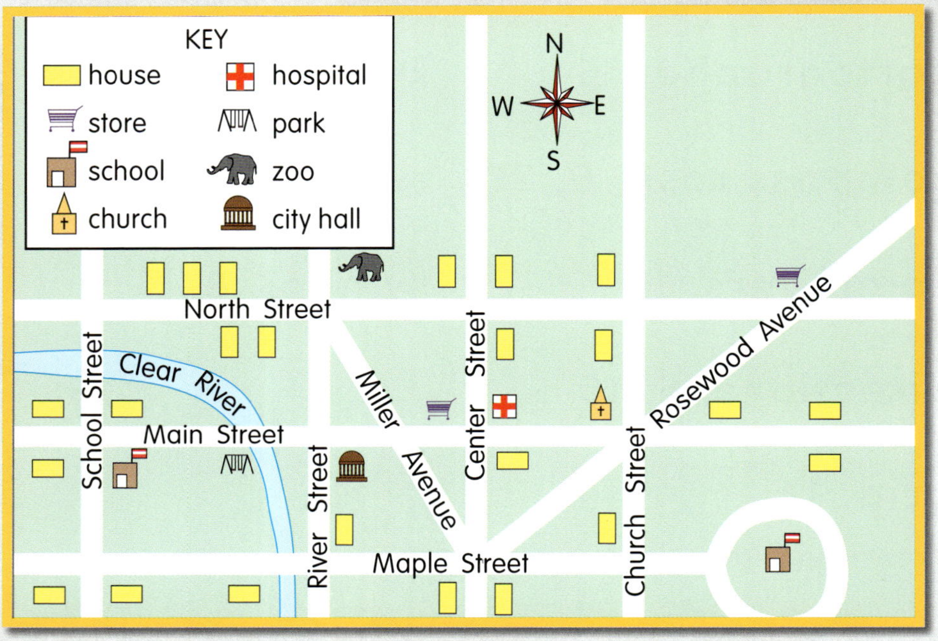

Can You Find It?

This map shows many places. It has a key to help you. Can you find a store? Can you find a school? How did you find those places?